ADOBE HOUSES

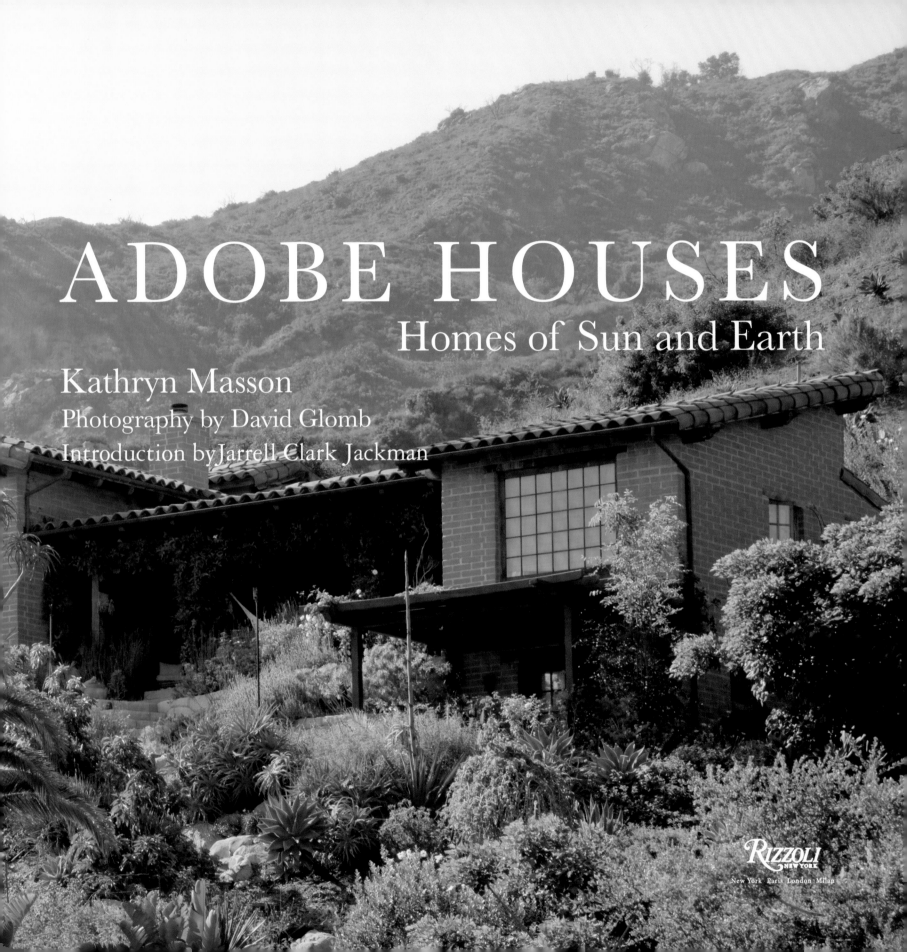

ADOBE HOUSES
Homes of Sun and Earth

Kathryn Masson

Photography by David Glomb

Introduction by Jarrell Clark Jackman

RIZZOLI
NEW YORK

New York Paris London Milan

First published in the United States of America in 2017 by
RIZZOLI INTERNATIONAL PUBLICATIONS, INC.
300 Park Avenue South, New York, NY 10010
www.rizzoliusa.com

ISBN-13: 978-0-8478-5844-6
Library of Congress Control Number: 2016952483

© 2017 Rizzoli International Publications, Inc.
Text © 2017 Kathryn Masson
Photography (unless otherwise noted) © 2017 David Glomb

Distributed to the U.S. Trade by Random House, New York

PAGE 1: *Casa Ashcraft, Santa Barbara*
PAGES 2–3: *Leo Carrillo's Rancho de los Quiotes adobe complex, Carlsbad*
PAGES 4-5: *In Casa del Oso's great room a window that soars to the high ceiling
and fills most of the front wall affords the interior with a magnificent view of the
surrounding Montecito hills.*
PAGES 6-7: *Casa del Oso, Montecito*

Designed by Abigail Sturges

Printed and bound in China

2017 2018 2019 2020 2021 / 10 9 8 7 6 5 4 3 2 1

DEDICATION

This book that is a brief history of adobe architecture of California is dedicated to Dr. Jarrell C. Jackman, long-time Executive Director of the Santa Barbara Trust for Historic Preservation (SBTHP). His success overseeing complex budgets, events, archaeological programs, myriad restoration projects, and fundraising has been phenomenal, and he leaves behind a legacy of having helped to grow SBTHP into one of the most financially healthy historical organizations in the state of California. During his tenure of three-and-a-half decades he lived and breathed adobes through his involvement and leadership in the rebuilding of the Santa Barbara Royal Presidio, the largest adobe reconstruction in North America, and the restoration of the 1820s Casa de la Guerra adobe mansion, both in downtown Santa Barbara. He has been a positive and creative force in the city of Santa Barbara and with state and national organizations whose responsibility it is to promote and protect California's built history. For his efforts in preserving and interpreting Spanish history in California and the American West, King Filipe VI of Spain has recently bestowed on Dr. Jackman one of Spain's highest honors: Commander of the Royal Order of Isabella the Catholic. He credits the intellect, support and great sense of humor of his wife, Michele, as the primary reasons he has been able to meet the many challenges he faced as a leader in the field of historic preservation. He now pursues research projects on hold for many years.

CONTENTS

PREFACE

The adobe architecture of early California is an essential part of our Western heritage. From existing eighteenth-century missions to the humble nineteenth-century one-room house, the presence of these adobe structures reminds us of the cultures that have contributed to California's diversity and strength today. The Santa Barbara Mission is majestic in its graceful setting opposite the city rose garden. And the other twenty missions that dot the California landscape from south to north are truly impressive in their now restored or reconstructed forms. Los Angeles, with a current population of nearly four million, is surreal when compared to its beginnings as a pueblo of 44 settlers less than two hundred and fifty years ago. In the heart of downtown Santa Barbara the decades-long and monumental task of reconstructing El Presidio de Santa Barbara progresses adobe brick by adobe brick. It is a striking site in the middle of a modern city.

Canet Hacienda, Morro Bay

But the buildings that seem to resonate the most with people today are the simple adobe houses built in the early nineteenth century by former presidio soldiers or their descendents in not-so-far-flung clusters near the presidios or as the cores of pueblos throughout California. They have an unmistakably sturdy quality due to their heavy bricks, thick walls, and a very real attachment to the earth. There is beauty in their natural materials. And quite often there is a visceral reaction of being held when inside the simple shelters.

Appreciation of California's adobes is a learning process. Experiencing the adobes first hand is an adventure. Although many of these historic adobes are now private homes, many have been restored and are maintained as public museums with furnishings that accurately present frontier life in the nineteenth century. Travel in Mexico and Spain reveals a landscape of towns and villages built in a vernacular that served as a precedent for our early California architecture. Adobes that include the twenty-one missions and those found especially in such places as Old Town San Diego, the earliest streets in Los Angeles, downtown Santa Barbara, the Historic District in Monterey, and around the Sonoma Plaza have been protected for future generations. The presence of the past is everywhere.

Our affinity with adobe architecture, however, goes beyond an appreciation of California's evolution during the Spanish and Mexican eras, and is rooted in our basic connection to the earth and hand craftsmanship. There is some allure, also, in the romantic mythological idealized form of the adobe house. Perhaps it is these nineteenth century adobes, inspirational in their restored forms, that guide those with a vision to contemplate building their own adobe homes.

Since there was no book concentrating solely on California's adobe history, one that showed the various forms of domestic adobe architecture was needed. Hopefully it will inspire designers, builders, architects, and homeowners to incorporate elements from these structures into the easy living of contemporary California homes. Here then are a selection of adobes—from early simple structures and elegant, commodious ranchero homes to the traditional and creative interpretations presented by builders from the mid-twentieth century to today.

INTRODUCTION

Jarrell Clark Jackman

Kathryn Masson is a longtime friend and I have admired the many books she has done on the architecture and cultural heritage in various regions in California and across the country in Virginia. But *Adobe Houses* has for me a special affinity, as the world of earthen architecture has been at the heart of my life for over half of it, even longer if I date it from the time when I first met my future wife, Michele. As a student at the University of California, Davis, she early on recounted how one of the most enjoyable experiences of her college years was living in an adobe house across from the campus: "There was something spiritual and welcoming about the house." Little did I know then that this was the beginning of an association with adobe that would become a dominant part of my life. As a kind of personal coda, I would visit many years later the town of Spišsky Štiavnik in Slovakia where my grandfather was born. I learned firsthand that he came to light on this earth in an earthen structure that still survives and remains a residence to this day.

Between the years 1967, when I met Michele, and 2015, I spent three and a half decades overseeing the conservation, restoration, and rebuilding of adobe structures in Santa Barbara, California, as the CAO and then

CEO of the Santa Barbara Trust for Historic Preservation (SBTHP). The work undertaken included the stabilization of El Cuartel, an original eighteenth-century adobe of El Presidio de Santa Barbara, the Spanish fort founded in California on April 21, 1782, and the last fort founded by the Spanish in North America. The massive presidio adobe defense wall (over four feet thick and over ten feet high) and its buildings encompassed a modern city block; it is estimated it required over 300,000 adobe blocks to complete. El Cuartel, which housed a Spanish soldier and his family, is the oldest surviving non-religious, domestic building in California, and thus the oldest surviving adobe residence in California, although today it serves as museum rooms as part of El Presidio de Santa Barbara State Historic Park.

SBTHP in collaboration with the California State Parks Department has been gradually rebuilding the eighteenth-century Spanish fort on its original foundations—to date having reconstructed eighteen adobe rooms, including the commandant's quarters, soldiers' family quarters, and the padre's quarters, not to mention the chapel. All told over the years, one hundred thousand adobe bricks have been made for these projects. Poured and molded in wooden forms from both imported soil and the dirt from archaeological excavations uncovering the original stone foundations of the fort, these bricks have been handmade mostly on site and each brick weighs around fifty-five pounds. About a third of El Presidio de Santa Barbara has been rebuilt to

LEFT

At Casa de la Guerra in Santa Barbara, covered raised porches lead to the separate entries of each room from the central courtyard. The thirteen-room adobe, known as "casa grande," was the most impressive residence in the small pueblo of Santa Barbara when it was built. The restored adobe now houses exhibits of the Santa Barbara Trust for Historic Preservation and is open on the weekends.

OPPOSITE

The 8,000-square-foot adobe mansion, Casa de la Guerra, was built from 1819–1826 for the family of Don José de la Guerra, the last Spanish commandant of El Presidio de Santa Barbara. It housed his large extended family and was the social, political and cultural center of Santa Barbara. It is a City of Santa Barbara and California State Historic Landmark and is listed on the National Register of Historic Places.

LEFT

The 1830 Lugo Adobe anchors the Meridian Studios, in downtown Santa Barbara, which were designed by architect George Washington Smith in 1923 as artists' studios.

OPPOSITE

Now in the backyard of a private Montecito estate, the one-room Dominguez adobe is one of only a handful of that area's remaining early-to-mid-nineteenth-century adobes.

date and there will be more to come in the future. Two buildings are original, the aforementioned El Cuartel and the Cañedo Adobe. SBTHP has been appropriately called "The Adobe Overlords of North America" and my daughter Renée describes me as "Dr. Adobe."

But the presidio is only one of the major adobe projects of the SBTHP. SBTHP owns Casa de la Guerra, built between 1819 and 1826 and the former home of Spanish-born Don José de la Guerra and his family. SBTHP has undertaken a major restoration of the adobe, which is around eight thousand square feet in size, and adjoins El Paseo, a Spanish Revival complex built in the early 1920s and considered to be the oldest shopping mall in California. SBTHP restored the Casa de la Guerra to its heyday period—1820s to 1858—meticulously restored I might add. Ninety percent of the restoration was based on physical evidence provided by above ground archaeology. For example, based on testing of original beams that had to be replaced, SBTHP harvested the same species of trees from the mountains above Santa Barbara—with permission of the National Forest Service.

For anyone interested in re-creating an accurate version of a nineteenth-century California adobe, the Casa de la Guerra would be a good place to start. Architect Cliff May is credited with perpetuating the Ranch House style of residences beginning in the 1930s based on his personal experience of growing up as a descendant of an early California family. While he had firsthand experience of his family residences, it turned out he based his designs on buildings that had been heavily restored in the early twentieth century and would be better described as Spanish Revival in style. Casa de la Guerra in turn captures the early-nineteenth-century tradition both on its exterior and in its interior.

During my long tenure as CEO of SBTHP, I learned a great deal about what is called "adobe technology"—I especially came to realize that what on the surface seems like a basic building material is, when "digging" into it, more complex than one first thinks. Basic adobe can be described as consisting of the four elements of earth, water, fire and air, with some kind of binder added to the mix. By this I mean an adobe brick consists primarily of silt, sand and clay (earth), is usually mixed with straw, and is then dried in the open air, under the natural fire of the sun. It is not baked or fired in an oven or kiln. More on the variants in a moment, but first just a little bit of adobe history.

Construction with adobe dates back to the early days of civilization in the Middle East (Babylon rose out of the ground using this building material) from whence it spread to and around the Mediterranean especially during the time of the Muslim Arab conquest that reached all the way to Spain in the eighth century. The word *adobe* is of Arabic origin. From The Iberian Peninsula, adobe architecture followed the Spanish and Portuguese to the New World, by the fifteenth century spreading southward into South and Central America, and northward to Mexico and to the Southwest region of North America under the rule of the Spanish—now Texas, New Mexico, Arizona and California.

An important education for me personally, regarding the history, various types of adobe construction, and its conservation came from attending and participating in two international earthen architecture conferences—one in Las Cruces, New Mexico, in 1990 and the other in 2000 at Torquay, England. At these conferences, attendees came from numerous countries—China, India, Saudi Arabia, Australia, Germany, Yugoslavia, Australia, and Peru, to name just some of the nations participating. There are various versions of earthen architecture—the traditional bricks, rammed earth, so-called pisé, and cob. Cob construction is a mixture of soil, with some sort of fibrous material as a binder, and is layered on walls rather than formed into bricks. The Torquay conference was held in southwest England because there are literally thousands of cob structures, many of them barns built in Devon and surrounding counties, mostly in the eighteenth century. Today many of these buildings are being "gentrified" and turned into residences.

It is estimated that as much as ten percent of the population of China lives in earthen structures—that is millions of people, obviously. There are some really surprising cases where adobe structures have been built. After World War II, several thousand adobe buildings appeared in Germany to house those who had lost their residences to the ravages of the war. Along the Hudson River, there were residences built of adobe in the eighteenth and nineteenth centuries. Today many of those structures survive in both Germany and New York.

On a trip in the 1990s to the birthplace of the eighteenth-century commandant of the El Presidio de Santa Barbara, Felipe de Goicoechea, in the town of Cosalá, in Sinaloa, Mexico, Michele and I discovered that almost all of the buildings of the town were adobes, using caning roofing material, layered with mud on which clay roof tiles were laid. In Santa Barbara, we have been rebuilding exactly these kinds of buildings (adding some reinforcement) but their purpose is to interpret and educate the public about California's early history; in Mexico, people still reside in these earthen type structures. Besides Mexico, there are strong domestic adobe traditions in many Latin American countries, especially Peru and Colombia.

One other enlightening trip to Mexico was to Guadalajara, with Kathryn Masson and famed architectural historian, Dr. David Gebhard. Underneath the plastering of many of its classical public buildings we noted chipped away sections that revealed the walls were made of adobe bricks! I wouldn't say that adobe construction is ubiquitous but it certainly exists around the world in places where one might least expect it, and as material in buildings that may not appear at all to be made of adobe.

The earthen building tradition in the American West leads first of all to New Mexico, which has the largest percentage of adobes of any state, some dating back to the seventeenth century. The Governor's Palace in Santa Fe is a fine example of an early adobe style that evolved into what is traditionally called the Territorial Style and is often copied in modern adobe construction there. The most prevalent style of architecture in New Mexico, however, is the Pueblo Style of the Native Americans.

California's built environment in its early years under Spanish and Mexican rule (1769 to 1846) was almost entirely constructed from adobe bricks, with only a few of the mission churches made of stone masonry. By the end of the Mexican period in Santa Barbara there were approximately two hundred adobe residences. Today only slightly over a dozen of those adobes survive. Fortunately, five of them are under the care and protection of SBTHP and California State Parks and most of the others fall under local landmark designation prohibiting demolition or untoward changes to them.

California, along the coast, has the right relatively dry climate for adobe, but it is in a significant seismic region, subject to severe earthquakes with which contemporary Californians are all too familiar. The earthquakes of 1812 were devastating to California's adobe buildings. With the aftershocks, going on for months, the Santa Barbara presidio soldiers and their families took up residence outdoors in tents until things settled down and repairs were completed. Thus, preserving and building adobes in California presents challenges. Adobes can be retrofitted as has been done at Casa de la Guerra. Even before a retrofit, the Casa survived two major seismic events, one in 1857 and

Rancho de los Quiotes was built as a retreat for actor, preservationist, and descendant of one of the founding Spanish families in San Diego, Leo Carrillo, from 1937 to 1939 on 840 acres he bought in Carlsbad. The retreat complex eventually grew to eighteen buildings, many of them adobe, on 2500 acres. Now the historic buildings and twenty-seven acres comprise the Leo Carrillo Historic Park, a California State Historic Landmark that is also listed on the National Register of Historic Places and open to the public.

another in 1925. The primary reason it came through these temblors intact, with the only major damage to the original porch that had to be replaced, was the extra thick walls of the adobe. In the building of the Casa from 1819 to 1826, Don José de la Guerra knew from past experience (he arrived in California in 1802) that his house would have to be able to withstand future earthquakes. In fact adobes with thick walls do quite well in earthquakes if kept to one story. Taller than that, the buildings are vulnerable to the perils of plate tectonics.

It is also important to keep in mind proper conservation and restoration techniques and treatments when dealing with adobes. The rule of thumb is always to use like materials. If the adobe is pure—that is, unamended without any use of cement or an oil-based material such as emulsified asphalt, then any treatment should only use unamended adobes and mud mortar. If there is some cement used in the mortar or the bricks then cement can be used in repair. Much damage has been done to early adobes by using cement plaster and replacing unamended with amended bricks. Building codes enforced by building departments these

days require some type of re-enforcement. In addition adobes can require significant maintenance. Basal erosion by what is called "rising damp" can damage a building. Moisture is not the friend of any building material, but it is particularly damaging to adobe.

Yet with all the challenges, there are advantages to adobe—one such often being the ability to make the bricks right on site from local soil. Natural insulation, though somewhat overrated, is another plus. But all said and done, there is something else at play in the attraction of many to living in an adobe. That is: The so-called romantic sense that this is the perfect type of construction for domestic bliss.

Building and living in an adobe house is a passion. The twenty-three adobe houses featured in this volume are all in California, spanning a period from the Spanish and Mexican eras all the way up to the turn of twentieth century. They are in most instances still lived in: and I would feel right at home in any of them. The simple adobe architecture allows its owners the latitude to furnish, decorate, and landscape to their individual tastes. The results have been stunning, powerful statements forged from a basic architectural style. The architect Louis Sullivan made the famous statement that "the building without reflects the people within"; in the cases of these adobes the buildings both without and within carry forth an ancient earthen building tradition dating back thousands of years, updated in some instances through advances in technology, but most of all they are homes that dreams are made of…. For those of us seeking models for our own future dream houses, the adobes that the reader will encounter in this book will provide inspiration of the first order.

CASA BORONDA

Monterey, 1818–ca.1820s

It was an ideal location overlooking the presidio and the church, with a spring-fed stream that flowed from the mesa to Monterey Bay, that attracted former presidio soldiers to this prime location on which reportedly two adobes were built by Boronda family members. One of those built by patriarch Manuel Boronda in 1818 no longer exists. According to author Dr. Julianne Burton-Carvajal, the surviving Boronda adobe was built a generation later by Miguel Allen, the Irish-born husband of Petra Boronda, Manuel's youngest daughter. The expanding number of adobes built outside the presidio walls would become the earliest core of Monterey. By the 1820s to 1830s, the adobes would form the nucleus of the port town, the port of entry for trading in Alta California, authorized by the Mexican government in 1822, and the capital, so named in 1776 and continuing as such until 1846.

Patriarch Manuel Boronda was a trained carpenter who had immigrated from Guadalajara, New Spain (now Mexico), and served as a soldier at El Presidio de Santa Barbara. To populate Alta California the Spanish government encouraged marriage and large families. In 1790, when he was thirty-nine years old, Manuel married thirteen-year-old Gertrudis Higuera Arredondo, thereafter relocating to the San Francisco Presidio. From 1782–1812, the couple had thirteen children, eight of whom would survive to adulthood.

Although the main room's tile flooring and fireplace are not original, they compliment the elements that are, such as the deep-set windows in the thick adobe walls and the exposed wood-beamed ceilings, to create a warm atmosphere along with the textures of leather, heavy fabric accents, and dark wood furniture.

By 1814, the Borondas had relocated to Monterey onto land granted by the Mexican government as payment for the former soldier's military service. Here, Manuel and, after his death in 1826, his son-in-law, built possibly two adobes, according to Burton-Caravajal, who states, "It would be safer to say that the existing home was possibly built subsequent to and slightly above the original. Because it was passed down through the widowed (and briefly remarried) Petra Boronda, it has always retained the name. Certainly the location corresponds to the first of the three casas Boronda in Monterey County." The Casa Boronda that exists today is a single-story, four-room (originally two-room) adobe. In it, or one nearby, the Borondas raised their large family. Generations often lived together, sometimes crowding up to fifteen adults and children into moderate homes. The existing Casa Boronda adobe would be owned by Boronda descendants until its purchase by Alexander Tiers in 1939.

After secularization of the missions began in 1833 allowing immigrants and residents to claim land, the Boronda clan dispersed across the California landscape. Some Borondas remained in Monterey County, building Casas Boronda in Salinas and Carmel Valley. Other members of the Boronda family moved to such places as Santa Barbara and San Diego.

In 1922, 1940, and again in the early twenty-first century, the casa underwent restoration and remodeling that honored its integrity and character. In 2000, the seven-acre property with the historic adobe was bought by a couple who wished to conserve and protect it from sub-division and commercial development. In this grand gesture, this sturdy and beautifully restored adobe and its unencumbered hilltop environment have been preserved for future generations as an irreplaceable part of Monterey and California's heritage.

ABOVE
The interior has now been divided
into more rooms that include the
main living room, the dining room
(shown here), the bedroom, a small
bathroom, an area with shelves
that leads to the kitchen, and the
kitchen. Rooms lead from one to the
other with doors on either side of
the spaces, as there is no hallway.

RIGHT
In the space appropriated for the
modern kitchen at the end of the
house, large cabinets painted a
vibrant red add even more cheer
to the bright yellow walls.

FOLLOWING PAGES
The bedroom, with a door that
leads to the landscaped walled
courtyard, is located between the
dining room and the kitchen. The
use of the color red, dark wood,
and authentic wrought iron accents
throughout the home compliment
each other as well as create earthy,
grounded interiors.

OPPOSITE

The many doors and windows are accented with color that contrasts sharply with the stark white of the adobe walls. Simple landscaping and this plain, beautiful architecture are striking examples of California's best and most enduring designs.

RIGHT

Shadows play a large part in the charm of an adobe house. The roofline, surrounding trees, nearby plants and exposed straight wood beams of a simple trellis play effectively against the surfaces of the adobe walls, leveled gravel, and well-manicured grass adding dimension to the structure's basic design.

GONZALEZ-RAMIREZ ADOBE

Santa Barbara, 1825

One of the most carefully restored adobe residences in Santa Barbara dating from the early nineteenth century (Mexican period) is the Gonzalez-Ramirez adobe. Sometime between 1825, when presidio soldier Rafael Gonzalez married Maria Antonia Guevara, and 1827, when he was discharged from the army, he built an adobe house on a plot of high ground above the then-present marshes and lagoon near the Santa Barbara Royal Presidio.

The adobe structure was set about a hundred feet from the edge of a hill overlooking the former lagoon. The one-room-deep, one-story residence was configured as a rectangle with its original entrance oriented away from the lagoon, looking toward the village of Santa Barbara and its center, El Presidio de Santa Barbara. Today the historic adobe is designated a National Historic Landmark, a City of Santa Barbara Historic Landmark, and is listed on the National Register of Historic Places.

Rafael Gonzales had grown up in Santa Barbara and in 1816 enlisted as a soldier at El Presidio de Santa Barbara. From 1817 to 1827, Gonzalez saw military duty at Mission Santa Inés, Mission San Buenaventura and Mission La Purisima. In 1827, he was discharged from the army and returned to Santa Barbara. He was Santa Barbara's alcalde in 1829, served as majordomo at Mission La Purisima in 1836 in charge of allocating former mission lands, and in 1838 provided this service at Mission San Buenaventura. In 1845, he again became alcalde of Santa Barbara.

Randall House Rare Books, one of the most eminent rare book dealers in the United States, has been located in the historic adobe since the 1980s. Visitors may browse rooms filled with fine and rare books, as well as historic documents and original artwork.

Rafael and Maria Antonia Gonzalez had seven children. In 1866, Rafael deeded the house and property to his three living daughters. One of them, Maria Solome Francisca Ventura, who married Cristobal Ramirez, lived in the adobe until her death. In 1923, David and Louise Murphy Vhay bought the property from Ventura's estate. Mrs. Vhay restored and enlarged the adobe during the next four decades, carefully maintaining its historic character. The adobe is now the business address of Randall House Rare Books, Ronald Randall, proprietor, where his period furnishings and abundant collections of fine books enhance the palpable charm.

Architect Louise Murphy
Vhay, who restored and
enlarged the adobe during
her four decade residence,
improved it with electricity,
gas heat, five fireplaces, two
bathrooms, and more doors
and windows.

CASA ABREGO

Monterey, 1835

Don José Abrego was granted a city lot in 1835 upon which he built his adobe residence. From it he ran a grocery store and soap making business. Later the successful Abrego's home became a social center of Monterey.

OPPOSITE
An enfilade leads from the front door through the house to doors that open to the private garden.

Don José Abrego came to Monterey in 1834 on the schooner *La Natalia* with a group of colonists who were relocating to California as members of the Cosmopolitan Company, an ill-fated attempt sponsored by the Mexican Government to populate the frontier of California. Setting sail from San Blas, Mexico, the passengers included 239 persons, of which there were 105 men, 55 women, and 79 children. The adults were educated and trained teachers, seamstresses, agricultural workers, artisans, midwives, and trades people such as Don José Abrego, a hat maker from Mexico.

In 1835, Abrego was granted a town lot in Monterey, the capital of Alta California and main port for all of California trade, a place with untold business opportunities. A year later he married Josefa Estrada, the daughter of a wealthy ranching family, and with that connection and his business acumen Abrego soon succeeded financially. He ran a grocery store and soap-making business from his adobe home. On one of his many other properties he ran a bar and billiard parlor. His 2,267-acre Rancho Punta de Pinos along the coast was granted in 1844 and he purchased Rancho San Francisquito in 1853. He also owned property in Yerba Buena (San Francisco). He held various civic and political offices, including Provisional Treasurer of Alta California from 1838–1846, and was one of Monterey's most prominent citizens. Because

The open plan of the sitting room and library, with tall ceilings and deep set windows in the thick adobe walls, is enhanced for modern use with wood trim work and built in book cases

of his stature in the community and his business connections, his sociable wife, and a thriving family with eleven children, the home became an important social center, made lively with music from one of the first pianos in California.

A century later, in 1956, the adobe was scheduled for demolition but was saved by the Monterey Foundation. The Abrego Club, a community member private club purchased the valuable adobe in 1959 and has been its meticulous steward ever since.

LEFT
The large room used for dining is well lit by a window installed by an artist who had a studio there in the early twentieth century. The elegant space is used for formal gatherings by the Abrego Club, the adobe's owner and steward since 1959.

RIGHT
A window in the library affords a view of the lush garden and bricked patio serving the house.

FOLLOWING PAGES
A high wall encloses the back garden designed by noted twentieth-century California landscape architect Florence Yoch.

CASA SERRANO

Monterey, 1840

The 1840 adobe contains a well-curated collection of furnishings and art that represent eighteenth- and nineteenth-century life in Monterey. Exhibits are rotated by the Monterey History and Art Association who own and have restored the adobe.

OPPOSITE
Florencio Serrano was a schoolteacher who held classes in his adobe. In the other room of the original adobe residence a nineteenth-century secretary holds books that represent a "lady's model library" of the period.

"Monterey, as far as my observation goes, is decidedly the pleasantest and most civilized-looking place in California," wrote Richard Henry Dana Jr. in 1835 in a journal of his voyage along the California coast from 1834–1836 that would be published as *Two Years Before the Mast*. He continues:

> … the town lay directly before us, making a very pretty appearance; its houses being of whitewashed adobe … the red tiles, too, on the roofs, contrasted well with the white sides, and with the extreme greenness of the lawn upon which the houses—about a hundred in number—were dotted about, here and there, irregularly. There are in this place … no streets nor fences … so that houses are placed at random upon the green. This, as they are of one story, and of the cottage form, gives them a pretty effect when seen from a distance.

A Chickering (Boston) square (or box) grand piano, one of the first in California and the same as one in the Lincoln-era White House, is the focal point of the large back addition to the original adobe. Over it is hung The Gossips, *an oil on canvas painted by important California artist E. Charlton Fortune in 1921.*

FOLLOWING PAGES
A bronze by cowboy and artist Jo Mora is displayed on a carved eighteenth-century Spanish table with stabilizing wrought iron cross bars. Above it a selection of Mora's pen and ink drawings. The Monterey History and Art Association owns the largest collection of publically displayed Jo Mora drawings, rotating in exhibits at Casa Serrano. Over the tufted black silk and horsehair settee, c. 1890s "untitled" (Casa Bonifacio), an oil on canvas.

One of the adobes added to this growing community, California's capital from 1776–1846, was Casa Serrano. The house was built in 1840 by Irish-American blacksmith John Chamberlain, who had arrived in Monterey the year before. In 1841, Chamberlain sold the house to Thomas O. Larkin, the wealthy merchant and U.S. Consul to Mexican Alta California, whose notable two-story, balconied house was nearby. Larkin added a third room to the single-story casa and brought the adobe up to date with wood floors and glass windows.

Florencio Serrano, who had arrived in 1835 with the Cosmopolitan Company bought the casa in 1846. He was a merchant, schoolteacher, and eventually the second alcalde of Monterey. Serrano married Rita de la Torre and raised six children in the adobe. The casa remained in the hands of the descendants until 1959, when the Monterey History and Art Association purchased and restored it. It serves today as a repository for a well-curated collection of early Monterey's art and antique furniture.

60

CANET HACIENDA

Morro Bay, 1841

The centerpiece of the 4,379-acre Rancho San Bernardo, granted by the Mexican government in 1840 to Vincent Canet, is this adobe mansion in present-day Morro Bay. Originally a U-shaped, two-room deep house surrounding a central courtyard, the structure has been modified through the years to serve its modern residents, yet remains evocative of California life during the Mexican period. The sturdy adobe is set beside a mountain where open space creates a vision of old California and where horse ranching is the essence of existence.

Vicente Canet, who built the large adobe, was born in Valencia, Spain, sailed into Monterey Bay in 1825, and remained there to become a soldier at the Monterey Presidio for twelve years. After marrying and living on his rancho in Salinas for fifteen years, Canet petitioned the Mexican government for a land grant near the ocean and was deeded 4,379 acres near San Bernardo Creek in 1840. The Canets raised their family of nine children in the fourteen-room adobe completed in 1841 by Native American neophytes from nearby missions San Miguel and San Luis Obispo. After Canet's death in 1858 his cattle ranch was divided up and passed to his wife and children. In 1865 the United States government officially confirmed the original grant to Vicente Canet. Estevan Quintana purchased the 4,379-acre ranch in 1874 and gave it to his son Petro as a wedding present. After generations of sub-division Pietro Righetti bought 1,300 acres and the adobe house in 1880. Current owner Jo Ann Jones is Righetti's great granddaughter.

Jo Ann has lived in the adobe for over thirty years, ever since
she inherited the historic house and 1,300 acres. She and her husband John W. Jones Sr. have raised their family in the Western tradition, heavily invested in their horse ranching enterprise. Rodeos
are a natural part of life. John Sr. is a world champion steer wrestler
and his son, John Jr., competing as a member of the Professional
Rodeo Cowboys Association, is a three-time world champion steer
wrestler. Members of the family have also competed in calf roping,
barrel racing, goat tying, break away roping, pole bending, and
roping. Today John Jr., his wife, Sherrie, and their daughters, Katie
and Shannon, train horses at their arena up the road. Horses are
still a part of the Jones' daughter Sandra's life also; she and her
husband Dan Eddleman raise quarter horses in Montana and their
daughter Mattie began competing at age eleven. Three miles south
of Morro Bay the Joneses' iron entrance gate with a cutout Western
motif exemplifies their lives and their ranch, a vestige of nineteenth-century California.

SALVADOR VALLEJO ADOBE

(Sonoma Plaza), Sonoma, ca. 1840s

The interiors of Jean Thompson's spacious rooms are filled with color, texture, and whimsy. Her noteworthy collections of modern and contemporary Mexican folk art, gathered over decades of widespread travel, represent her love and celebration of the culture

The Salvador Vallejo adobe facing the Sonoma Plaza has a rich and complex history. Up to this day, sections of the building have served numerous purposes. It was conceived as a single-story adobe to be used as commercial space or possibly the town hall by Salvador Vallejo, the brother of General Mariano Vallejo, who was once the most important man in Sonoma and the most influential man in California. The adobe was begun in the early 1840s, possibly as early as 1843. It ran for 160 feet along the west side of the plaza, bisected by a large entrance passageway, with a hundred-foot section connecting at a right angle that faced West Spain Street, off the plaza. In the early 1850s, an adobe second-story addition was begun over the south section and a frame second story over the north section. In 1850, the north half of the building from the passageway became the mayor of Sonoma's offices and town council meeting rooms, but in 1851 all of this section became the El Dorado

Thompson juxtaposes
contemporary pieces, such as
Frank Gehry bentwood chairs,
a Ron Mann lamp, and
textural pillows by designer
Louise Mann with an antique
pine dresser and sideboard.

To the left of the fireplace is
a work of Outsider Art by
NIAD Art Center client-artist
Harry Ingram. The ceramic
figure on the green metal table
is by Cerrapio Madrano.

Hotel. In 1852, the large section south of and including the main passageway was used as a Masonic Hall. From 1858 to 1866, the whole adobe was used as a college that gave the building its Greek Revival facade. In 1866, the southern portion was used by vintner Camille Aguillon and, in 1890, the northern half again became a hotel. The 1906 earthquake ruined the hotel, but in 1908 proprietors rebuilt and reincarnated the El Dorado Hotel, which is still in existence today. Throughout its long history the massive two-story building has been a landmark on the Sonoma Plaza and is one of the few remaining original adobes from the Mexican era in Sonoma Valley.

Appropriately, Jean Thompson, an avid collector of Mexican art and a floral designer, resides in second-floor rooms of the southern section of the huge Salvador Vallejo adobe building. Her home includes a wide hallway, used as a gallery space, and two main rooms, each feeling larger than they are because of their eleven-foot-high ceilings. Short staircases lead from the hallway up to the framed doors of each of the two rooms, a parlor and a bedroom, which are filled with Thompson's colorful Mexican art collections.

Thompson first visited Mexico in 1963, traveling to Mexico City, Tasco, and Acapulco. Then in 1964 when she and friends stayed in Puerta Vallarta, she began her decades-long infatuation with and collection of Mexican art. Later, she and her late husband traveled extensively in Mexico, adding to their carefully curated collection. Thompson still discovers new places in Mexico, but has found the states of Michoacan, Oaxaca, and Jalisco to be the richest for crafts. Thompson advises that repeating, or grouping items has more impact than one of this and one of that. Also important are folk art themes, such as watermelons, angels, and skeletons. She truly leads an artful life, surrounded with pieces that please her everyday and enliven her historic home.

The bed, designed by
Louise Mann, with
multicolored embroidered
fabric from Oaxaca, is
surrounded by angels,
wings, and hearts. On her
wall are a paper art dress
on hanger, a metal wire
web, a Rameno Andrade
pastel of an angel, and
magenta woven reed beads.

BOESEKE ADOBE

Santa Barbara (Montecito), 1845

The Boeseke adobe as it stands today incorporates modifications made beginning in 1916 by Herbert C. Cox, a polo enthusiast, who also built a polo complex nearby. Later, the adobe became a clubhouse for the Polo Club when it was owned by Elmer J. Boeseke Jr. Its sweeping wide verandas show a romanticized ideal of nineteenth-century California adobes.

When the Mexican government began to secularize the missions in 1833, vast tracts of land were granted to settlers and former soldiers from the four presidios in California. Montecito, located adjacent to Santa Barbara to the southeast, began with small adobe houses clustered near what is now the upper village as well as adobe houses built for recipients of land grants. In 1845, Nemecio Dominguez, the son of a retired soldier from El Presidio de Santa Barbara, was granted 356 acres in this area. He called his property Rancho San Leandro and reportedly built two adobes from which to run a cattle operation and crop farm on a small portion of the property. These structures may have been constructed as early as 1835 or 1836, and may have been incorporated in the existing adobe, but no definitive proof exists.

The Dominguez family lived on the ranch through 1868, when the many changes of ownership and division of the ranch lands began. Records are not conclusive, but reportedly in 1880 James H. Swift bought the ranch and with his father further developed and expanded the ranching enterprise. The Swift's ranch included 150 acres planted with flax, hay, barley, corn, fruits and vegetables as well as 300 olive trees. In 1887 Swift sold 240 acres to A.L. Anderson, who in 1888 transferred the title to George H. Gould. It appears that Swift's two brothers continued to manage the ranch from a farmhouse they had built ca. 1881 until it was sold.

The great room includes a sitting area and a dining area, and is anchored at each end by a massive fireplace. High ceilings with heavy wooden trusses create an elegant space for McHugh's superb antique furnishings and richly textured fabrics.

Herbert C. Cox renamed the ranch Ennisbrook when he purchased 120 acres from Gould in 1916. He restored and may have enlarged the historic adobe and resided there with his wife. Polo was popular among the elite of Santa Barbara and Montecito at the time, and in 1923 Cox improved the site with a polo complex that included a playing field, the third in Montecito, a practice ring, three stables, and a multi-use guest house-stable building.

One of the men who played polo on Cox field was Elmer J. Boeseke Jr., who would become a Bronze Medalist on the 1924 U.S. Olympic Polo Team. In 1926, he bought Ennisbrook and further improved the polo complex, enlarging the stables for 150 horses. He also remodeled and may have expanded the historic adobe, which he used as a part-time residence for himself and his wife, and later as a clubhouse for the Polo Club. With the Depression and WWII, interest in polo waned and the once vibrant polo fields deteriorated. Boeseke died in 1965. In 1986, two developers, one of whom refurbished the historic adobe as his residence, created a planned community, Ennisbrook, on 120 acres of the original ranch.

The Boeseke adobe is a treasure in the elegant Ennisbrook. It now anchors a nearly six-acre estate, improved by owner Deanna McHugh from 2000 to 2016 with a Monterey Colonial-style farmhouse, a four-stall stable of sympathetic mid-nineteenth-century design, a nearby riding ring, and a manicured garden accented with Santa Barbara sandstone pathways.

ABOVE
The master bedroom is well-appointed
with sparse but beautiful antiques. Deep-
set windows trimmed in dark wood that
show the substantial thickness of the
adobe walls add character to the room.

OPPOSITE
Deanna McHugh improved the six-acre
estate with a Monterey Colonial
Revival–style farmhouse.

FOLLOWING PAGES
The improvements made by horse
enthusiast McHugh from 2000 to 2016
included a four-stall stable of sympathetic
mid-nineteenth-century design, a nearby
riding ring, and gardens with pathways
of Santa Barbara sandstone that lead to
the adobe residence.

RAY ADOBE

Sonoma, 1847

*Tall columns that hold the
roof of the Ray adobe are
repurposed ships' masts from
various vessels abandoned in
San Francisco Bay during the
gold rush era. An elegant
wide hipped roof protects the
painted adobe walls. Many
flowering plants in the
gardens at the front and side
of the adobe include Spuria
Iris and Damask roses
planted in the early 1930s.*

OPPOSITE

*An interior remodel in the
1850s by the U.S. Army
enclosed the back veranda to
create a mess hall. Today the
long space is used as a gallery
walkway with a dramatic
fourteen-foot high ceiling.*

Built on former mission lands near the Sonoma Plaza, the Ray adobe is one of only a handful of existing two-story nineteenth-century adobes in California. It is owned by architect Ned Forrest, who is also a preservationist active with the Blue Wing Trust in Sonoma, and his wife, Leslie Whitelaw, an interior designer formerly based in Arizona. The couple brings an acute sensibility and expert knowledge of adobe buildings to the stewardship of their handsome and historically significant residence.

Constructed in sections over time, the house began as a simple wooden two-story structure built by John and Harriett Ray in 1847. After their short but successful venture in the gold fields, they returned to their home in Sonoma where they used earth from a neighboring lot to make adobe bricks and complete an impressive two-story adobe addition. In 1851, their neighbor Lewis Adler bought the house made from his lot's dirt for $4,000. The adobe's early history includes its use as a boarding house and officers' mess for soldiers under Captain Brackett, U.S. Army, during the gold rush in the nearby hills. In May 1851, the Sonoma Masonic Lodge was chartered here. Meetings were held during the years 1851–1865 and in the early years Lt. William Tecumseh Sherman was a member. Incarnations as a railroad warehouse, an antique shop, and a tearoom followed.

Remodels of the interior began in the early 1850s, when the U. S. Army enclosed the back veranda to create a mess hall and added an interior staircase to access the

LEFT

Interior designer Leslie Whitelaw used a custom-blended complex warm gray-brown color for the living room walls in keeping with the adobe material of which they are made. The earth tone of the linen upholstery fabric creates a subdued backdrop masterfully complimented with touches of vibrant green.

RIGHT

In his office at the far end of the living room, Forrest uses a desk converted from a nineteenth-century piano. There is no better view from the many windows and doors along the adobe's main facade than the bucolic country scene a stone's throw away.

From one of the doors on the main facade you enter a small room that opens to the dining room at one end and the living room at the other. The stark white paint of the wooden trim work has been subdued with glazing.

FOLLOWING PAGES
In the dining room traditional furnishings include ladder-back chairs and a polished cherry table Forrest's parents found in rural Kentucky in the 1950s. A color palette was developed matching colors found in adobes in Monterey and Santa Barbara.

second floor. Today the long space is used as a gallery walkway with a dramatic fourteen-foot high ceiling. A remodel in 1940 included a two-story wooden addition and conversion of the second story living spaces. Later, Forrest retrofitted the house and removed materials from 1960s and 1970s remodels. The adobe now shows elements from its history during the 1840s through the 1940s.

Forrest and Whitelaw have lived in their adobe through earthquakes, including one in 2014, repairing the damage of "cracked plaster walls, but nothing more major, thankfully." Maintaining the health of the edifice with such improvements as a new roof and fresh coats of paint is paramount. The interior design is evolving according to the couple's principled conviction of remaining true to the essence of the original adobe, with the addition of strong, warm, earth-toned paint colors for walls. Whitelaw explains that the use of complex, blended colors, such as the soothing pink-brown in a bathroom or the warm grey-brown in the living room, as well as the glazing of the wood trim throughout the house to subdue its stark white paint harmonize the spaces and affirm the strong sensory phenomenon felt inside the rooms. "Being inside a thick-walled adobe house gives you the feeling that you are being held. Masonry and adobe buildings have an ability to do that. It's inherent in their properties," Whitelaw concludes—a wonderful description of a warm and heartfelt living experience.

OPPOSITE TOP
The sunny master bedroom is found on the second floor of the two-story 1940 wooden addition.

OPPOSITE BOTTOM
A claw foot tub, pedestal sink, comfortable side chair, and an antique wooden quilt stand with woven cloths for towels complete the well-appointed bathroom.

RIGHT
A guestroom accessed from an interior staircase and balcony that runs along the length of the interior built during the 1850 remodel once served as the meeting room for the Sonoma Masonic Lodge, chartered here in 1851. Members met from 1851 to 1865.

CASA DE LA TORRE

Monterey, 1851

Casa de la Torre, built ca. 1851 on a third-of-an-acre corner lot, is one of the few privately owned original adobe residences in Monterey. The original three-room house with an entry hall was probably the work of Francisco Pinto, who had received a land grant in 1850 that was assessed at $7.50. The grant stipulated that a residence be built on the land within two years, so on June 21, 1851, when Pinto sold the property to Juan Bonifacio the price had increased to $150 and a structure most probably had added value.

In 1862, the adobe was purchased by José Remigio de la Torre, the youngest son of Don José Joaquin de la Torre, who was one of the most prominent men in Monterey, a civic leader with strong political ties, including serving as secretary of Governor Alvarado in 1848. Because his father was the grantee of two large ranchos nearby, received in 1822 and 1840, José de Remigio most probably grew up on one of them. He became a rancher.

In 1862, however, José de Remigio and his wife Guadalupe Holjin moved into town, acquiring the adobe in which they would raise their five children. It is reported that seven generations lived in the house over more than half a century.

The house has been changed with several owners. One of the first non-family owners of the adobe was Myron Oliver, a local painter who bought it in 1924 and knocked out the majority of the north wall to install a huge arched window, thereby making the main room a well-lit artist's studio. Now at 2,100 square feet, the casa still embodies the architectural character reflective of the early Monterey adobes. It is a valuable part of the Monterey Old Town National Historic Landmark District.

A large arched window was cut out of the thick adobe wall in 1924 when Monterey artist Myron Oliver converted the main room into his studio. California art is featured on the walls of the comfortable room and the metal chandelier that centers the dining table leads the eye up to the high wooden-beamed ceiling that gives the space volume.

Adobe walls left unadorned,
painted in a warm white
reveal the character of the
sturdy structure.

OPPOSITE
*The kitchen has been deco-
rated with colored glazed
tile and a hood designed to
blend with the undulating
surface of an adobe wall.
Owners use all manner of
Mexican glazed ceramic
canisters, bowls, plates and
mugs to further embellish the
kitchen and continue the
Mexican theme.*

A simple, sculptural staircase at the back of the great room leads to the small loft space.

OPPOSITE
Varied roof lines and chimney heights add interest to the peaceful private patio and garden that has been beautified with plants appropriate for the California climate.

ARRELLANES-KIRK ADOBE

Santa Barbara, prior to 1852

A low wide veranda covering the front porch and protecting the natural adobe walls, together with a lush garden, create an inviting and well-conceived entry that is a visual step back into nineteenth-century California.

The Arrellanes-Kirk adobe is set, like the Gonzalez-Ramirez adobe, on land rising from the marshes and lagoon that have now been filled in with city streets in downtown Santa Barbara. From the street a steep bank leads up to a level pad upon which the Arrellanes-Kirk adobe was built. A low wide veranda covering the front porch and a lush garden create an inviting and well-conceived entry that is a visual step back into nineteenth-century California.

There is no record of who built the original approximately thirty-eight-by-seventeen-foot adobe house, so theories abounded and written reports in 1972 and 1982 surmised its date as the mid-1850s or late 1860s. Finally, the 2004 Historical Structures Report by Post/Hazeltine Associates and Alexandra C. Cole of Preservation Planning Associates definitively dated the construction of the adobe as no later than 1852.

The two families that were the adobe's early owners, the Arrellanes family and the Dominquez family, are prominent in the history of eighteenth- and early-nineteenth-century California's founding and development. Barbara Dominguez Arrellanes was the recorded owner from February 1868. Both Barbara's paternal grandfather and her husband Francisco's father had been founding soldiers at El Presidio de Santa Barbara.

Patriarch Teodore Arrellanes was a prosperous presidio soldier by 1798 when he built the first of his adobes on property he owned around the presidio. He was awarded large land grants by the Mexican government, including the 4,428-acre

Architect Allen Zimmer's improvements of the historic adobe included modifications such as removal of three twentieth-century wooden additions and building a one-story wing to enlarge the residence for contemporary living. He also added a triangular piece over the side window for interest.

Rancho El Rincon (1835) in eastern Santa Barbara County and the 43,683-acre Rancho Guadalupe (1840) in San Luis Obispo and Santa Barbara Counties. The family wealth came from cattle ranching, providing tallow and hides to the East Coast, and beef to the '49ers.

By 1868, the Arrellanes family's successful ranching enterprises had decreased because of the drought from 1862 to 1865, but nonetheless, Francisco purchased the whole city block on which the adobe stood. He then sold a portion of it in 1872 to his daughter Angustias and her husband Francis Kirk. After they made it their residence, it is surmised that Kirk, who was a carpenter, revised the adobe's design with wood-framed windows, a wood and glass front door, weatherboard siding, and the addition of a wood structure (after 1878). The Kirks lived there until 1886, the year Francis died. The adobe was then sold out of the Arrellanes-Kirk family. The series of owners that followed maintained the original adobe's integrity with a few additions and adequate maintenance.

In 2002, J. Allen Zimmer, a well-known architect in Santa Barbara, purchased the adobe, and in 2007 completed modifications that preserved its historical character while addressing issues important for contemporary living. His major work included an entire re-roofing, removal of three twentieth-century wood additions while maintaining the small, late nineteenth-century wooden addition, and building an appropriate one-story wing at the northeast corner of the adobe to replace an existing wing.

The Arrellanes-Kirk adobe is a City of Santa Barbara Historic Landmark and is listed on the California Register of Historical Resources as well as the National Register of Historical Resources.

ANDRONICO VALLEJO ADOBE

Sonoma, 1852

Included in the seven-acre property is a sizeable vineyard in front of the 1852 adobe set among mature trees, with a backdrop of the Sonoma hills. Dormer windows were added to provide light into the family's private living space in the upper floor.

Andronico Antonio Vallejo, eldest son of General Mariano Guadalupe Vallejo and Francisca Benicia Carrillo de Vallejo, was born in 1834. He lived until the age of sixty-two, dying in early 1897. In his lifetime, which spanned the Mexican into American eras in California, he saw many changes to the culture of his native Sonoma. He was raised in the wealthiest and most socially prominent family in northern California growing up in the general's Casa Grande, an imposing two-story mansion that faced the Sonoma Plaza. It was a large household; the Vallejos had sixteen children, ten of whom grew to adulthood. General Vallejo's home became the celebrated social center of northern California.

During the Mexican era marriages were made among the leading approximately one hundred families in California to solidify the value of their lands and maintain the cultural status quo. Andronico never married. His artistic temperament sepa-

The dining room was modified in the 1930s restoration with build-in bookcases and a set of large windows. The fireplace is part of the original adobe.

FOLLOWING PAGES
A simple plan includes parlors on each side of the spacious entry foyer with a staircase to the upper level, and a short hall leading to what is now a bedroom, the dining room and kitchen. The house now includes a family room. Finely carved wood trim throughout the house is original.

rated him from normal expectations and possibly caused a rift with his father.

The adobe home and barn that became Andronico's on land near the plaza are thought to have been built by John Ray in 1852 and sold to Mrs. Vallejo in 1853. She gifted the property to her favorite son hoping that he would settle close to home. Since Andronico's return from school in 1855, he had unhappily worked in the fields and lived at his father's final home, Lachryma Montis, a small house that the general's diminishing circumstances had behooved him to move into. After moving into his new adobe home the artistically natured Andronico raised crops on his land and that of his father, until in 1860 he moved to Vallejo to live a quiet existence as a music and languages teacher, his true passion.

Ironically, the home of a single man became a lively social center with the Smiths. In 1974, the seven-acre house and grounds were purchased by the current owners, whose family lineage may be traced to the Abregos of Monterey. Here they raised their family and now entertain their grandchildren, seventh generation Californians. The Olympic-size pool, tennis court, and party room on the second floor of the large barn have been perfect for the many social gatherings through the years.

The guest bedroom on the main floor has a minimum of furnishings that create a peaceful space.

FOLLOWING PAGES
The backyard of the house includes a trellis-covered patio, lawn area, and rose garden. Adjacent to this fenced space are found an Olympic-size swimming pool, tennis court, and a huge original barn with its upper floor converted to a party and game room, much used by friends and family through the years.

HAYS-LATIMER ADOBE

San Luis Obispo, prior to 1866

Double doors open from the living room, part of the 1885 addition that adds another thirty feet to the length of the current home, to the fresh air and a lush, mature garden planted by owner Dave Hannings, Professor of Horticulture at Cal Poly /San Luis Obispo. Collections of international artwork, sculpture, ceramics, and textiles from such places as Mexico, Argentina, and South Africa, enliven the interior.

FOLLOWING PAGES
Hannings chose a warm cantaloupe orange and green paint palette for the weatherboard exterior. Improvements to the property include paving the front walk and porch with colored Mexican pressed concrete tiles in a one-hundred-year-old pattern. Magnolia and peach trees, flowering plants, such as Heleconia, camellias, roses, and Wisteria, succulents, and vegetables, such as tomatoes and squash are grown in various gardens.

This adobe house, built a short walk from the Mission San Luis Obispo de Tolosa and facing Montgomery Street, is sheathed in weatherboard and painted in welcoming earth tones of cantaloupe orange and green. Dave Hannings, Professor of Horticulture at Cal Poly/San Luis Obispo and the historic residence's owner since 2001, has filled the interior with a riot of color with his choice of exciting paint and his eclectic displays of international art, including glazed Mexican vases and tile, West African and Mexican masks, textiles from around the world, and two antique French fireplace surrounds embedded with fossils. He takes pride in his restored house, lively interiors, and magnificent gardens, periodically welcoming visitors on home tours.

Although some adobe structures were coated only with a layer of mud, some were better protected from the weather by lime plaster washes, and later, after milled wood became available in the 1840s, by sheathing the buildings in weatherboard.

A ten-foot wide entrance hall is an enfilade reaching twenty-nine feet from the large entry door to the double doors between the end of the hallway and the living room that signifies the back of the original adobe. The original adobe, comprised of three rooms configured into a square, includes the hallway and what are now the master bedroom, bathroom, and dining room spaces.

FOLLOWIWNG PAGES
The wall connecting the vibrantly blue painted dining room to the kitchen would have been the back of the original adobe. A newly designed kitchen that uses appropriately historical materials and a sunroom now connect to the dining room.

In Hannings' adobe, a truth window, a small glazed window that is framed within the wall to show, in this case, a portion of an exterior adobe wall with some original plaster coating and a portion of the wood lintel is found over the door from the dining room to the kitchen. "This wall is the back wall of the original adobe," Hannings explains, "that was three rooms configured into a square." One side wall is the exterior wall of his ten-foot by twenty-nine-foot entrance hallway, also made of adobe bricks. As reported in *Vignettes of History in San Luis Obispo*, by Louisiana Clayton Dart (1978), the current hallway, bedroom, bathroom, and dining room are the original space of the adobe home. The adobe is situated on grounds reported to have been the mission's olive orchard, land that was sold off by 1850.

An important civic leader who previously occupied the adobe was Dr. W. W. Hays, a Union Army surgeon during the Civil War who relocated his family to the mild, healthful climate of San Luis Obispo in 1866. He became an outstanding member of the small, mostly Spanish and Indian community that was an early stagecoach stop halfway between Los Angeles and San Francisco. Perhaps it was he who enlarged the house into eight rooms

126

From the front entry a ten-foot wide hallway reaches the full length of the original adobe that would have ended at the double doors between the hall and living room.

and updated its appearance with the current Victorian style. He would have had the means, as he ran a thriving practice.

Dave Hannings is a passionate adobe owner who has contributed a great deal of time and funds to remodels that have enhanced the historic structure. His work has included an Italian wrought iron fence that benefits the front stone wall and paving of the front walk and porch with colored Mexican pressed concrete tiles in a one-hundred-year-old pattern. His most recent contribution has been a complete rebuilding of the kitchen using historically appropriate materials and the addition of a sunroom. The luscious garden in the back and maintenance of the 125-year old wisteria in the front are also among Hannings' priorities.

TORRE LINDA

Santa Barbara (Montecito), 1924

The entry foyer exudes the elegance that continues throughout the house. The home was designed and built by Santa Barbara sculptor David Gray Jr. as the centerpiece of a nearly nine acre estate in Montecito, adjacent to the Graholm Estate, his family's home.

FOLLOWING PAGES
The forty-seven-foot water tower built in 1924 to serve Graholm was connected in the new design to a rectangular adobe structure with a wooden portion that featured two Monterey-style balconies.

Torre Linda is well situated on the crest of a hill with views of the Santa Barbara foothills to the east and the Pacific Ocean to the west. A long elegant drive, planted with Italian cypress on either side, leads to the entrance of the house. The home was designed and built by Santa Barbara sculptor David Gray Jr. on approximately nine acres of land he inherited from his mother in 1931. On this parcel, once part of the Gray family's thirty-acre Graholm estate, was a forty-seven-foot water tower, built in 1924. The design conceived for the home connected the water tower with a new adobe structure in the form of a rectangle 29 feet by 155 feet, with a wooden portion that featured two Monterey-style balconies. Together with these features and three-foot thick walls allowing deep reveals for the windows, the design reflected the 1930s interpretation of a nineteenth-century California adobe.

David Gray Jr. was the eldest son of Martha Platt Gray and David Gray Sr., who had been regular visitors to Santa Barbara from Detroit. In 1919, Gray Sr. sold his

A large informal dining space adjoins the kitchen. The thick stuccoed walls, dark wood accents, and antique furnishings give the interior a luxurious warmth.

FOLLOWING PAGES
The entry foyer leads through a new arched opening to the living room that was formerly the master bedroom. A locally sourced sandstone fireplace surround and mantel, special detailing on the dark wood crown molding, and gleaming richly stained hardwood floors create interest in the well-proportioned space.

stock in the Ford Motor Company, of which his father had been a founding investor, for twenty-six million dollars and moved his family to Santa Barbara. Architect Roland F. Sauter built the family the grand manor house, Graholm, on prime acreage amongst other large estates created by wealthy Midwest and East Coast transplants. David Gray Jr. grew up in this exciting atmosphere. David Gray Sr. became one of Santa Barbara's most influential philanthropists among a small group of like-minded millionaires who greatly transformed the community in the early twentieth century. They organized and financially supported such improvements as a new art museum, beachfront land for public use that became Chase Palm Park, and, after the 1925 earthquake, the relatively quick rebuilding of their town in the Spanish image, spearheaded by civic leaders Pearl Chase and Bernhard Hoffmann. Gray Sr. helped establish the Architectural Review Board and fund community drafting rooms where architects completed residential and commercial designs that resulted in over 2,000 building permits issued in record time. The Gray family legacy includes the tremendous civic work at a crucial time in the community's development, as well as two outstanding architectural structures, Graholm, now the home of the Brooks Photography Institute, and the private residence Torre Linda.

Beside a large glazed and metal window that overlooks the estate grounds toward the Santa Barbara foothills, the rough-cut sandstone of the fireplace surround and mantel give the corner a cozy, rustic charm.

OPPOSITE
A guest room that is exquisitely decorated with a crystal chandelier and French fabric also has a tall ceiling of heavy wood beams and a wood-burning fireplace to enhance the gracious space.

EL CASERIO

Santa Barbara, ca. 1930

From the circular drive that serves the cottages of El Caserio, a rustic wooden door and adobe wall covered with creeping fig guard the patio and entrance.

OPPOSITE

Inside the surrounding wall a private brick-paved patio at the entrance to the ca. 1948 adobe house is a perfect area for small gatherings, like those that took place among the bohemian artists who lived in the first studios of El Caserio in the 1930s.

One of the most charming, private, and coveted places to live in Santa Barbara is El Caserio, a cluster of nine small houses, mostly built in the Spanish Colonial Revival style with the exception of one adobe. Envisioned as an artists' enclave, a knoll in downtown Santa Barbara was developed beginning in the early 1930s by wealthy Michigan transplant Anna Louise Murphy Vhay and her husband, John, who moved to Santa Barbara in 1919. Mrs. Vhay was an architect and designer who was passionate about saving the historic adobes in Santa Barbara. El Caserio was located near Mrs. Vhay's home, the remodeled Gonzalez-Ramirez adobe and her studio.

A portion of the former land of presidio soldier Juan Cordero was subdivided into nine lots for John Vhay, a violinmaker, in 1930. His wife, Anna, designed the first two studios in El Caserio for him. Soon other lots were sold to artists that included two violinists and famed California landscape painter John Gamble. Next, architect J.J. Plunkett built his studio. The small group of dwellings captured the ambiance of early California and the residents enjoyed the friendly, creative, bohemian lifestyle.

Remodeling or building in El Caserio, dubbed the Greenwich Village of Santa Barbara, subsequent residents (overlapping in time) included photographers, sculptors, painters, and a nationally known furniture designer. In the 1950s, prominent Santa Barbara ranching families, the Pedottis, Hollisters, and Peakes made El Case-

From the kitchen, French doors open to the patio and a series of arched openings lead from the kitchen through the living room to the private living quarters of the house. Owner and interior designer Micholyn Brown completely gutted the adobe and renovated it, featuring brick flooring, freshly painted white walls, and a second floor, for which she was honored with the 2009 Santa Barbara Beautiful Award for single-family residence.

rio their in-town abodes. Architect Lutah Maria Riggs, the partner of prolific Santa Barbara architect George Washington Smith, remodeled four of the original studios for the Hollister family. More current residents who continue the artistic tradition at El Caserio are Wendy Foster, whose four women's clothing stores define chic style, Pierre Lafond, owner of the Santa Barbara Winery among other enterprises, and Jill Sattler, an artist and jewelry designer.

In 2008, interior designer Micholyn Brown undertook an extensive remodel of the ca. 1948 adobe studio of professional photographer J. Walter Collinge Sr. She gutted the adobe house then improved it with new infrastructure and a second floor. Brown's exceptional work won the Santa Barbara Beautiful Award in 2009 for single small family residence.

The home showcases such features as tall ceilings sheathed in dark wood, deep-set windows, and fully rounded arched openings between rooms. Plain white walls and a simply designed fireplace are essential elements for subtle California glamour.

OPPOSITE
Brown enlarged the adobe during the extensive renovation with a second floor that includes an additional bedroom

CASA ASHCRAFT

Santa Barbara, 1932

The interior courtyard of Casa Ashcraft is an inviting space whose gnarled olive trees and sloping veranda throw shade on rustic wooden furniture meant for relaxing. Adobe walls are adorned with decorative hand-wrought ironwork and window openings are secured with roughly hewn wooden spindles.

The stunningly rustic adobe wall that faces a street near the heart of downtown Santa Barbara and is embellished with a decorative seventeenth-century Spanish iron grill over a colorful stained-glass window is the north facade of a spacious hacienda-style home. A further section of the continuous exterior wall that slopes to pedestrian level is punctuated by a single, hefty hand-carved wooden Mexican Colonial door that welcomes visitors into the enclosed private courtyard, enhanced with olive trees planted nearly a century ago, and the entrance to the residence.

The house sits on land once owned by Michigan transplants David and Anna Louise Murphy Vhay, who began buying and restoring a number of nineteenth-century adobe houses in this Santa Barbara area in 1923. In the 1930s, while they were developing El Caserio across the street, they sold this parcel to Bobby Hyde, who added a simple warehouse in 1932 and, later, a small cottage. In the 1950s, the

A brick floor laid in a basket weave pattern, a chimney breast that emulates the historic designs of the early proponents of Spanish and Mexican domestic architecture, and a wooden ceiling with dark-stained trusses that are original to the 1932 warehouse, are all made of natural materials that form the outstanding elements in the living room.

warehouse became a four-plex, and, after 1975, was remodeled, incorporating the small cottage, into a single-family residence. In 1996 when interior designer Micholyn Brown and her husband, Fred, bought the property their remodel was extensive, beginning with a re-landscaped brick courtyard anchored by the beautifully gnarled olive trees and enhanced with a Mexican fountain. The remodel continued with the addition of a master bedroom suite. The interior, casual yet elegant, has crisply whitewashed plaster walls that simulate the interior of an adobe house and play off the antique brick floors. High ceilings with stained wood and exposed trusses of the original warehouse add a relaxing breadth of space, while two fireplaces, one also original to the 1932 warehouse, warm the living room and dining room spaces.

Since 2006, when Lynn and Wayne Ashcraft relocated from their larger Santa Barbara home to this downtown sanctuary, they have enjoyed the comforts of twenty-first-century conveniences in the atmosphere of a Mexican Colonial-style California hacienda, where doors from every room open onto the private courtyard patio. The house has been honored with status as a City of Santa Barbara Structure of Merit.

The fireplace between the
remodeled kitchen and the
living-dining area is
original to the 1932
warehouse. It is unusual
and interesting as well as
functional.

OPPOSITE
A stained glass window
allows a brilliant spectrum
of colors to glow on surfaces
in the front bedroom.

The rustically whitewashed adobe facade in downtown Santa Barbara is well known for its charm. Everyone wants to know what's inside. And inside there is the courtyard and adobe hacienda-style home that hearken back to the romanticized life of Mexican-era California.

CASA CORAZON

Sonoma, 1938

A substantial veranda with carved wooden balusters is a shady spot from which to view the raised front garden full of drought tolerant and flowering plants.

OPPOSITE

A path leads from the back patio through a landscaped area beside the house where a Mexican fountain, potted plants, and comfortable seating provide a respite from the cares of the world.

In 1938, Frank Pensar, a Sonoma high school teacher, decided to build an adobe home as it would have been done a hundred years before. Sonoma is rich with some of the most important nineteenth-century adobes in California. The monolithic Petaluma Adobe, now Petaluma Adobe State Historic Park, was the ranch house for General Vallejo, once California's largest landowner. Other buildings include the barracks, the Blue Wing Inn, the Ray adobe, the Andronico Vallejo adobe, and the Salvador Vallejo adobe building, some of which have been meticulously restored.

In the spirit of handmade craftsmanship and in the tradition of California's first adobes, Pensar began making and drying adobe bricks from the clay-rich soil of his property. Reportedly, he was aided by some of his high school students and members of the community who rallied around the project. The house, with its long, low veranda that stretches the length of the front facade and faces the street with a planted garden in front, is a well-executed representation of California's historic architectural past.

The adobe had not been maintained for a while when it caught the attention of Bob Thorup, an experienced general contractor, who bought it in its "fixer upper" condition in 2005 intending to make it a showplace. Again, the adobe received the care of a man who valued fine craftsmanship and was enthusiastic about the adobe heritage of California. Thorup became well versed in adobe design and construction to complete the remodel. Extensive work included a new roof, extensive plumbing repairs, and replacement of rotted floors. New windows, doors, and beams were

Warm lighting from the table lamp's dimming shade, together with the honey-toned interior wood shutters and a the hefty iron chandelier, work with the patterned sofa, reminiscent of a woven Indian blanket, to give the living room a cozy Western vibe.

crafted to continue the historic style, and lintels and trim work were stripped to reveal the rustic raw wood. Thorup's creativity made use of an abundance of colorful glazed tile work in the kitchen and bathroom, as well as on a back patio entertainment area embellished with a built in barbecue, seating, and a Mexican fountain.

When the current owner bought the house in 2012, she was delighted with its transformation and committed to maintaining its uniqueness. It is now her sanctuary away from the workaday bustle of San Francisco.

Decorative wood beams and carved molding against a ceiling washed in color and the brick fireplace with inlaid decorations are the focal points of the living room.

OPPOSITE
Kitchen surfaces are covered with colorful hand-made glazed tile, walls are painted in lively bright colors, and a variety of highly decorated and patterned Mexican ceramics fill the shelves.

A peach palette of decorative glazed tile is used thoughtfully in the master bathroom.

OPPOSITE
A pattern of complimentary green and yellow tiles surround the back patio's stone wall fountain and decorate its base.

FOLLOWING PAGES
Colorful glazed tile dominates the patio/BBQ area. The fun area enclosed at the back of the house contains a raised tiled floor where a magnificent BBQ is decorated with unusual green glazed tile. Even the risers of the few steps leading to a slightly sunken sunny eating area are embellished with patterned Mexican tile.

RANCHO DOS ALISOS

Santa Barbara, 1939

The popularity of adobes is connected with our strong human bond with the earth, our appreciation of California's Spanish and Mexican eras, and the romance that surrounds their mythologized ideal. Nineteenth-century adobes still exist in many towns in California. It was not until the sawmill and the construction of wharfs in California's coastal towns that lumber became the standard building material and frame houses replaced adobes as the main architectural form. By the 1860s, few adobe buildings were still being constructed.

After the Mexican government ordered the secularization of the missions in 1833, the associated buildings became ruins. In places like Santa Barbara the creation of a grid system of streets in 1851 built over the existing haphazard placement of adobes meant that many of these homes were abandoned or demolished.

In the late teens and early 1920s, however, California's architectural heritage caught the attention of individuals who valued the historic adobes and wanted to save and restore or remodel them with modern amenities such as electricity and heat. Some historic adobes were saved while others continued to be demolished by city planners.

In 1939, Fredrick and Ann Booth moved from Pasadena and purchased the nineteenth-century Arturo Oreña adobe in Santa Barbara's foothills from his daughter, who was the great-grand daughter of Spaniard Don José de la Guerra, the fifth commandant of El Presidio de Santa Barbara and town patriarch. Unfortunately unsal-

The traditional adobe house, built on a prime hilltop location, was well designed with ample space in the backyard for relaxing and entertaining. The brick-paved veranda, furnished with groupings of Mexican chairs, settees, and tables, opens to a large paved courtyard-entertainment area. A swimming pool completes the scene. From anywhere in this expanded living area views of the Pacific Ocean and Santa Barbara may be enjoyed by all.

vageable, the Oreña adobe was razed and the Booths built a traditional adobe residence in its place. The foundation is three feet of river rocks and the bricks were made with clay soil from the property. The large U-shaped hacienda, finished in 1940, was kept in the family, with the Booth's daughter Betsy and her then husband John Woodward, California history enthusiasts, living there for several years.

Subsequent owners have always loved living in the elegant home that rests on nearly six acres. A gracious veranda at the entry typifies a distinguishing element from the early ranch houses, while a courtyard at the back is oriented toward an unequalled view of the city and Pacific Ocean beyond.

A huge divided window affords views of the finely landscaped property from the dining room. Heavy wood beams and a substantial iron chandelier add depth to the space.

OPPOSITE
Displayed on a carved wood sideboard are ceramic urns from Tlaquepaque, Mexico, and antique silver candlesticks. The California landscape painting by Whitney Brooks Abbot of Rincon Hill looking northwest to Santa Barbara has earth tones that compliment the items below.

*An unusually wide entry hall
foyer opens to a living room of
generous dimensions that amply
holds the owners' art, antiques,
and seating. A large window
opens to the backyard scene.*

*The master bedroom was de-
signed with the best views in
mind. A corner fireplace adds
warmth to the comfortable space.*

*The courtyard, veranda, patio,
pool, and ocean view comprise
the ideal California backyard
setting.*

RANCHO ZARA

Fallbrook, San Diego County, 1946

The adobe bricks of Rancho Zara in San Diego County are covered with a slurry coat. The exterior contains such design elements as protruding wood beams and traditional vegas just below the flat roof that release rain water. An unusual design for the large windows has them placed with rough cutting through the adobes surrounding them.

FOLLOWING PAGES

Rancho Zara is a modern estate that uses the Pueblo style of the American Southwest to convey California lifestyle sensibilities. It was designed and built from 1946 to 1952 with twenty-seven thousand adobe bricks that were hand-made on the hilltop site.

Ranacho Zara is a work of art. The architecture together with the landscaped gardens and patios presents a cohesive whole, a modern estate that uses the Pueblo style of the American Southwest to convey California lifestyle sensibilities. The rich visual displays presented inside and out demonstrate how these early forms and artifacts may be brought together for twenty-first-century living in Southern California. The exterior design and its execution, the interior decoration and its details, and the various patios and grotto are as intriguing and welcoming today as they were when the adobe home was completed.

Owner Breining's father bought the mountain-top 170 acres on which this house was built inland from San Diego with a 360-degree view of the surrounding countryside. He began laying brick in 1946 with the assistance of his son Michael, then sixteen. Twenty-seven thousand adobe bricks, all made on site, were used in the sturdy structure that has withstood earthquakes and fire. Today, Michael and his wife Nancy are now the sole occupants of the secluded retreat.

The Pueblo style adobe includes identifying design elements such as visible adobe bricks sometimes plastered but here covered with a slurry coat, vegas protruding from just below the flat roof that release rain water, and steps built into the side of the house that are both practical and artistic. The immediate landscape

License was taken with the design to allow for larger windows that let in needed light to the low-ceilinged rooms. In the living room, a collection of Native American and Mexican art and artifacts, silver jewelry, and woven textiles, as well as the adobe walls, tiled arch openings, and rough-hewn wood ceiling beams are highly decorative.

FOLLOWING PAGES
Silver concho belts hung on the wall as a display against a Native American hand-woven rug, one in the owner's fine collection, a Mexican-style pressed-tin mirror frame, rustic hand-made Mexican glazed tile, woven baskets, and California paintings create a powerful Southwestern ambiance in the living room.

includes two patios with gardens that contain cacti and other drought tolerant plantings befitting a semi-arid climate.

Rancho Zara décor showcases the owners' private collections of Native American and Mexican artifacts, silver jewelry, art, and woven textiles. These pieces remind Michael of his affinity for Mexico and the American Southwest. His fascination with Mexican culture began when living as a child in Mexico City and Guadalajara, and continued while studying at the National University in Sonora, where he was part of a team that restored a 250-year-old adobe ruin. The Breinings' life has been an adventure few have lived. Now they are settled in a house and surroundings that take them to a peaceful existence in the American Southwest.

A stuccoed corner fireplace with stepped hearth in the living room and the one in the dining area where bricks are left untouched are traditional design elements of the Southwestern style.

OPPOSITE
A Mexican starlight pendant light with a decorative bracket spreads a pattern of shadows on the white adobe walls. Sturdy pine logs with bark removed are used as ceiling beams as well as bracing elements for an additional counter space.

A wooden door is carved with the Native American "River of Life" pattern. The hand-wrought iron door pull is a custom design.

RIGHT
A bedroom is simply furnished but with painted closet doors and decorative iron hardware for added interest.

A door with a patterned
window inset opens to the
back patio and garden.

ABOVE AND OPPOSITE
One of the practical yet
artistic features of Pueblo
style architecture are the
exterior steps that give access
to the rooftop, often used as
a patio area.

HACIENDA GUADALAPANA

Santa Barbara (Montecito), 1947

A niche in the wall facing the courtyard at Hacienda Guadalupana holds a whimsical clay statue.

OPPOSITE

An arch in the adobe wall that surrounds Hacienda Guadalupana welcomes visitors to the adobe house built by Bob and Winni Bennett with bricks made by hand on site.

Bob Bennett grew up in Chula Vista, then a small California town that bordered Mexico, infatuated with the culture and romance of Mexico. He wished to live in an adobe house, years later becoming the driving force for a building project that took seventeen years to complete. The simple beauty of this vernacular architecture had captured his heart and his main desire was to emulate the beloved culture of Mexico in his life.

In 1947, youth, energy and a vision led the newly married Bennetts (Bob and Winni), then living in Southern California but familiar with Santa Barbara, to buy land in Montecito onto which they aspired to build an authentic adobe house. Bob had found Winni to be a willing partner in the endeavor. The plan would be a traditional Mexican design of three one-room-deep, one story structures connected in a "U" shape with a courtyard in the middle. Originally the couple wanted many

Bob Bennett's vision of an authentic Mexican adobe home was realized after nearly two decades beginning with the purchase of a three-quarters-of-an-acre lot in Montecito in 1947. From 1953 to 1955, thousands of bricks were made for the home that would include three bedrooms, two baths, a large living room, and a kitchen with a dining area.

acres, but the real estate market being what it was even in the 1960s, they found a smaller but appropriate three quarters of an acre for $2,000, originally part of a larger historic late-nineteenth-century estate. Their plan was to make the adobe bricks as well as build the house themselves. Their lot provided good dirt for the adobes, correctly proportioned with clay and sand.

In the beginning of the project, 6,500 adobe bricks were bought from Peter Aguilar, a local adobe builder who, with his brother, ran an adobe making facility located in downtown Santa Barbara. The remainder of the many thousands of bricks were made from 1953 to 1955 by the Bennetts. The southern section of the house was finished first, housing the family. When the estate was completed it contained a substantial adobe wall surrounding a picturesque house with three bedrooms, two bathrooms, a large living room, and a kitchen with a dining room.

Together, Winni and Bob raised six children while the handmade house was under construction. Bob's enthusiasm for building the adobe never wavered, though he was a husband and a father, and worked full-time in Santa Barbara. He admirably stuck to a strict schedule, building from five to seven in the morning before work, then from five to nine in the evening. In reaching his goal after almost two decades, he not only provided his family with a unique and beautiful home, but gave his children a rich appreciation of the Mexican culture.

One of the bedrooms shows the adobe's simple design that uses painted wood doors and stained wood for high vaulted ceilings and unfinished wood closet doors.

RIGHT
The spacious living room opens on one side to the entry foyer with a hallway to bedrooms and on the other to the kitchen and dining area. A huge window with a low tiled seating area provides a view of the courtyard with its fountain and many potted plants.

FOLLOWING PAGES
Sturdy adobe piers hold the tiled veranda roof that shades the three sides of the U-shaped house around the central courtyard. The paved courtyard is a much-used living space.

CASA ROBINSON AGUILAR

Santa Barbara (Hope Ranch), 1950

Tim Aguilar, a professional adobe maker and builder, and his wife, Susan, have displayed Southwestern artifacts and art in the niches and patios of their Hope Ranch, Santa Barbara house. Sets of antique wooden doors from New Mexico were also used in the exterior design of the house. The Aguilars' collections add an authentic rusticity to the background of adobe walls.

Tim Aguilar is a professional adobe maker and builder. The knowledge and skill are almost part of his DNA. His grandfather was a stonemason who worked on the carved sandstone seen bordering the roads from the Santa Barbara Mission to Sycamore Canyon Road. Tim's father, Joe, and uncle Pete were builders and adobe makers by trade, owning and operating the adobe brickyard located on Gutierrez Street on the east side of Santa Barbara. They often worked with architect Lutah Maria Riggs. Adobe homes in Montecito and Santa Barbara built by them from the 1940s through the 1960s are iconic examples of the genre. Since the 1970s, Tim, a graduate of the California College of Arts and Crafts in Berkeley, has carried on his family's tradition by making and building homes with adobe bricks. One of his main activities has also been to supervise brick making for the Santa Barbara Trust for Historic Preservation, the organization whose mission it is to rebuild the eighteenth-century El Presidio de Santa Barbara. In addition, he is the "go to" man when the property owner of a historic adobe needs advice and reconstruction help.

One of the most recent projects that Tim has managed is the restoration and reconstruction of the historic Hosmer adobe in Montecito. For years it stood with its wooden outbuildings, vacant, on a prominent rise, visible to the upper village. The new buyer was the perfect person to honor the nineteenth-century adobe

Aguilar has been converting the original stuccoed house, built by his wife's parents in 1950, into a full-brick adobe structure. A tile roof was also added. With a 2,000-square-foot adobe addition, the now 4,800-square-foot ranch house has been transformed into a style that evokes early California.

and the estate. She knew to hire Tim to bring the adobe back to life.

Tim and his wife, Susan, live in Hope Ranch in Santa Barbara, in a California ranch house that her parents built in 1950. Tim has been converting the originally stuccoed house to a full-brick adobe structure with a 2,000-square-foot two-story addition that includes a workshop/studio below with an office and gallery space above. A tile roof was also added. The now 4,800-square-foot, mid-century ranch house has been transformed to a style that evokes early California. An antique wooden double gate purchased in New Mexico guards the entrance to the one-hundred-foot driveway and at the house another set of antique wooden gates leads to the garage and workshop. Freestanding adobe walls delineate the main entry. Susan's collection of Southwest baskets adds authentic flavor to the home while wooden furniture, desert skulls and other Southwestern antique objects d'art accent the outdoor spaces.

CASA O GOLDMAN

Santa Barbara (Montecito), 1989

High above the city, perched on forty acres in the Montecito hills, the adobe home that was completed in 1989 is a testament to the tenacity of its owners. Their winding driveway alone took an entire year to complete. Stone piers on a low stone wall add a unique look to the adobe structure.

FOLLOWING PAGES
Steps form the veranda lead to an infinity pool with landscaped gardens on either side. With the nearby hillside as a backdrop, the stone and hand-made terra-cotta roof tiles blend with the natural scene.

Set high on the top of a mountain overlooking a landscape thick with California chaparral and the distant Pacific Ocean, Casa O Goldman is a love story and a journey. It is the reality of a dream that David Goldman and Shan O'Brien Goldman had had since the early 1980s when they had bought forty acres in Montecito on which to build a spacious adobe home. Returning home to a sanctuary would be an exciting comfort after extensive travels to global destinations.

Shan's concept for the house was realized by Santa Barbara architect and civil engineer Howard Wittausch. "He understood my design ideas and translated them into a strong technical structure," explains Shan. Well-known adobe builder Gordon Gibbons also collaborated early on with some architectural details. Elements from the places the couple had visited were incorporated into the architecture, giving it a character deserving of their vast collection of global treasures. The Goldmans moved into their new home in 1989.

The adobe is a result of passions followed and well-planned lives. David's master plan was to combine his two great loves, food and travel. He studied journalism at the University of Southern California, then became a real estate developer to make the money needed to spend the rest of his life writing. He wrote the "Opinionated Traveler" column for the *Montecito Journal* and a weekly nationally syndicated column that was carried in 155 newspapers by the Copley News Service. David had a

Rare and beautiful treasures from the owners' world travels are displayed behind glass. Among them are, on the right side, from the top shelves down: a Chinese ceremonial headdress next to a child's ceremonial dress; in the center of the second shelf is a vintage Balinese dancing headdress; and on bottom shelf are Omani tribal headdresses made of goatskin and beads that still smell of campfire. On the shelves to left of door are a silver horse bridle and vintage Hmoung headdresses.

FOLLOWING PAGES
A sophisticated sitting area opens to the dining area where a filigreed Moroccan lantern hangs above the carved wood table that seats twelve, designed by the owner. Found below a Richard Ross photograph is a seventeenth-century Portuguese birthing bed covered in tangerine velvet. Other diverse international decorations include amber trade beads from Niger, camel saddle pillows (under the coffee table), a kilim rug, and a vintage Japanese kimono.

refreshing perspective. "Markets were a big thing for him. He loved neighborhoods, not the touristy places," says Shan. And in many of the global spots they visited, Shan's more visual orientation and artistic nature led them to unusual objects d'art, paintings, textiles, and furniture that now enhance the interiors of the casa with a definitive international flavor.

A voluminous space for the dining area that flows easily into the kitchen was designed with massive wood trusses holding the eighteen-foot ceiling.

FOLLOWING PAGES
Built after the main house was finished, a two-story guesthouse was designed with architecture sympathetic to the adobe structure. The large room on the second floor serves as a guest bedroom and library. The armoire is made of antique Omani doors.

LEFT

The master bedroom's centerpiece is a Mission Revival style bed covered with a handmade Hungarian gypsy cloth. A silk quilt enhances the chaise lounge. Beside the antique Mexican blue armoire is an Irish schoolmaster's desk.

ABOVE

Ever artistic, as she deadheads spent blooms in her rose garden, Shan throws them into her beehive oven, a common shape in Africa.

FOLLOWING PAGES

What a magnificent view from the veranda!

JACKALOPE RANCH

Sonoma, 1990

One of the six miniature donkeys that live at Jackalope Ranch, the home of Dave Whiteley and his wife, Chris Finlay, guards the adobe wall front entry.

OPPOSITE

A vine-covered veranda is a shady entry for the adobe designed and built by Dave Whiteley over a three-year period beginning in the summer of 1990. After becoming a certified adobero, he enlisted his two sons and many of their friends to make thousands of 30-pound adobe bricks.

FOLLOWING PAGES

The 840-square-foot adobe house was built on the footprint of a long-gone farmhouse, on eighteen acres of the original Dowdall family tract of 1850. Two sets of walls were built eight inches apart to accommodate conduit and rebars.

Dave Whiteley, owner of Dave Whiteley and Sons Construction, and his wife, Chris Finlay, share their eighteen acres at the base of the foothills in Sonoma Valley, originally part of the Dowdall family tract of 1850, with their horses and miniature donkeys. Their adobe residence is built on the footprint of a long-gone farmhouse, with a clear water creek running beside it, and a former early twentieth-century garden's iris, roses, and oleander still in bloom.

"Adobes are part of Sonoma's culture and climate," explains Whiteley, who was inspired by the renovation of the Sonoma Barracks and his experience living in the nearby Blue Wing Inn opposite the Sonoma Mission. He thereafter spent several years researching adobe building, including attending school in Albuquerque to become a certified "adobero" (an adobe builder). Work making several thousand bricks began in the summer of 1990 and continued for three years, mostly in summers when the heat could dry the adobe mud. Whiteley enlisted his two sons and usually six to eight of their teenage friends to mix mud and fill the wooden molds, producing, when thoroughly dried, adobe bricks that measured 8-by-16-by-4 inches and weighed 30 pounds each. After many thousands of bricks had been made, four Mexican adobe masons built a mammoth foundation six feet wide and several feet deep for the 840 square foot house. Then the exterior walls, each actually two sets of adobe walls, 10 to 14 feet high and 24 inches thick, were spaced 8 inches apart

A *tall ceiling in the living room adds volume and makes it feel spacious. The dining area and kitchen are on one side of the main room with bathroom and bedroom on the other. Flooring is terra-cotta pavers throughout. Rustic wood furniture, a display of Native American arrowheads, and leather sofas compliment the unfinished adobe walls and unglazed floor tiles.*

so that conduit could be run and cement poured into the space already strengthened with rebar. The earthquake proof adobe took three more years to complete.

Mud material consisted of fine particles that came from screened grindings of rock from Nuns Canyon Quarry in Glen Ellen. Bricks of various colors resulted from material taken from different areas and different years. Grinding of opelite, for instance, produced fine particles of a golden color known as Sonoma gold. Some dark brown, commercial bricks from Hans Sumpf in Madera were also used.

The design is pure: there is no finish paint, siding or trim. The siting is perfect: the bedroom faces east to capture the morning light, while the front porch faces south for good light throughout the day. From the porch in the evening, Whiteley and Finlay watch the adobe bricks turn a calming rosy color. Perfect.

A raised garden with plots contained in low adobe walls were the first to be built. A separate wall surrounds the garden.

FOLLOWING PAGES
One of the many horses on the ranch sneaks a drink from the water fountain in the front yard. The porch is the perfect place to enjoy the evening light turn the adobes a dusky rose.

RIGHT
Whiteley, owner of Dave Whiteley and Sons Construction, built a smaller adobe across from the residence for use as an office.

CASA DEL OSO

Santa Barbara (Montecito), 2000

Owner and designer Diana Lackner has given the interior a special energy with her expertly painted scenes and designs. Here a door with brilliant bright colors pops against the cobalt blue painted stucco wall.

OPPOSITE

Tom and Diana Lackner's adobe, into which they moved in 2000, is still a work in progress. The 3,000-square-foot residence has two levels. Below the main floor where the living room, dining room/kitchen, den, bedrooms, and bathrooms are found, Tom, a musician and recording engineer, has a studio and office. A guest suite is also part of the lower level.

Tom and Diana Lackner's hillside adobe home in Montecito overflows with happiness and joy. That's because they enjoyed the process of building it themselves (with seasonal help from their son and daughter, friends of their friends, and neighbors) over the three years it took to get it finished enough to live in while they still worked on it. Tom, a musician and recording engineer, can recall conversations he had while placing certain bricks. The house is abundant with great memories and personal touches. Its interior is a bright celebration of their love of traveling the world and of Diana's artistic talent. Artistic by nature, she nurtures her passion by seeking out unusual textiles, ceramics, and objects d'art wherever she travels and by decorating the surfaces of their casa with her painting. She is also responsible for the colorful glazed tile work designs throughout the house. The interior is a work of art in itself. Cheerful and exuberant!

Tom had grown up watching friends of his parents, such as Frank Robinson, Bobby Hyde, and Bill Neely, the first generation of adobe builders (who also grew their own vegetables and stomped their own grapes for wine) in Montecito after WWII, build their community of hillside adobes. "Fifty dollars down, fifty dollars a month, and a handshake," is how Tom remembers Bobby Hyde's $2,000 lots were sold. So after remodeling a number of houses in Santa Barbara, and with the inspiration from the past, Tom and Diana were ready to buy the nearly four-acre lot and give adobe building a try. They broke ground in 1997, and, thousands of bricks later, in 2000, the house was habitable. Their creative work is ongoing today.

Diana had conceived the design of the house but consulted with architect and life-long Santa Barbara resident Jeff Shelton on changes that would bring the plan to realization. The 3,000-square-foot house has two levels: on the main floor are the living room, dining room/kitchen, den, bathrooms and bedrooms, and a sweeping veranda with doors that open to the interior; below are Tom's music studio, an office, and a guest bedroom.

The Lackners had purchased their parcel when it was lush with fresh green growth from the rains. But in 2008, the Tea Fire raged in the hills and destroyed many of the hand-built adobes from the 1940s and 1950s, erasing that bohemian part of Santa Barbara's history forever. Casa del Oso however was spared but in a "moonscape" setting, as Diana describes it. Through hard work and dedication their surrounding landscape is healthy once again with beautiful gardens that complement the earthy house. And the Lackners continue to refine their unusual home with embellishments from every corner of the world.

The intense blue is repeated with effect behind the shelving in the wall niches. Colorful rugs, tile, ceramics and pillow fabric fill the space with good cheer. A guest bedroom loft over the entry hall looks out onto the living room through an intricately carved wood screen.

OPPOSITE
The Lackners have filled their home with colorful art, striking sculpture, a selection of woven textiles, and ceramics, collections from their extensive travels abroad that have included Mexico, Cuba, Peru, Chile, Argentina, Cambodia, Vietnam, India, and Bali. Diana's artistic flair includes her painted design on the unusually shaped chimney in the living room.

LEFT

Warm wood dominates the guest bedroom/loft overlooking the living room in the ceiling and heavy beams, and the intricate wooden screen used for privacy.

ABOVE

In the master bedroom the raised bed has a headboard and footboard built from carved doors from India. To use the space under the high bed, large drawers were built, which were then embellished by Diana. She often changes the textiles accenting furniture, including this pieced bedspread.

FOLLOWING PAGES

A sweeping veranda spreads the full length of the house. It is decorated with mementoes from the couples' travels (not the least of which are beautiful embroidered textiles), and comfortable furniture (including a hammock) that completes the inviting outdoor living space. An unparalleled view through the Mexican blood vines includes nearby mountain terrain and the Pacific Ocean beyond.

ACKNOWLEDGMENTS

Warm thanks are offered to the following individuals and institutions (all in California, unless otherwise noted), whose support, encouragement and information proved so helpful in the writing of this book:

Tim Aguilar, adobe construction, Santa Barbara

Beach Alexander, architectural designer, Sonoma

Tomas Bollay, architect, Thomas Bollay Architects, Inc., Santa Barbara

John Burk, Treasurer, Monterey History and Arts Association, Monterey

Julianne Burton-Carvajal, Ph.D., author, professor, Monterey

Mick Calarco, Special Project/Historic Sites Manager, City of Carlsbad Parks and Recreation Department, Carlsbad

Karin Campion, architectural designer, Andrew, Clarke, Chase, Chip, Sonoma

Cristiano Colantoni, former Curator of Collections and Exhibits, Monterey History and Arts Association, Monterey

Kim Cole, Principle Planner, Town Manager, City of Monterey

Dennis Copeland, historian; Museums, Cultural Arts and Archives Manager, City of Monterey

Robert and Leslie Demler, California Heritage Society, Sonoma

Helen DiZio, Rancho Santa Fe Garden Club, Rancho Santa Fe

Ned Forrest, architect, Forrest Architects, Sonoma

Juan Francisco, interpreter, Degollado, Jalisco, Mexico and Marshall, Virginia

Michael Green, Interpreter III, Program Management, California State Parks, Monterey State Historic Park, Monterey

Carol Grimes Gartland, reference, Solana Beach

Danna Gunther, research, Solana Beach

Ruth Gunther, reference, Solana Beach

Don and Joyce Hulsebos, Santa Barbara

Jarrell C. Jackman, Ph.D. CEO and Executive Director Emeritus, Santa Barbara Trust for Historic Preservation, Santa Barbara

Michele Jackman, author, corporate executives trainer, Santa Barbara

Dabrina Kahn, Santa Barbara

Leo Carrillo Adobe, Rancho de Los Quiotes, Carlsbad: Skip Moyer, docent; Sarah Kelly, administration

Larry Loyd, Sonoma and Mexico

Dana and Renee Longo, Santa Barbara

Luna Rustica, San Luis Obispo

Jana-Louisa Matheson, Casa Boronda, castellana y proprietor, Monterey

Mission San Luis Rey, Oceanside: Maureen Sullivan, Director of Public Relations; Jack Rodriguez, Property Manager

Pia Oliver, assistant, Randall House Rare Books

David Pashley, American Bird Conservancy, The Plains, Virginia

Petaluma Adobe State Historic Park, Petaluma

Kris Quist, District Museum Curator, Monterey District, Monterey State Historic Park, California State Department of Parks and Recreation, Monterey

Ron Randall, proprietor, Randall House Rare Books

Michael Redmon, Director of Research, Santa Barbara Historical Museum, Santa Barbara

Laurel Roberts, Laurel Roberts Equine Design and Consulting, Salinas and Santa Ynez

Jeanie Sturges, event coordinator, Monterey State Historic Park, Monterey

Maureen Sullivan, Director of Public Relations, Mission San Luis Rey, Oceanside

Christie Tam, research, Monterey

Bob Thorup, contractor and Cindy Osborn, The Entrepreneur's Source, Port Angeles, Washington

Nick Walker, interior designer, Sonoma and Mexico

Leslie Whitelaw, interior designer, Forrest Architects, Sonoma

Jeanne Woolridge, interpreter, Pacific House, Monterey

In special thanks, I extend my gratitude to all of the adobe owners who graciously opened their homes for inclusion in this book. And to our friends, without whose hospitality this book would have not been possible. All around great photographer and friend David Glomb, who took the outstanding images shown within this book for everyone to enjoy, deserves major praise. It is always a pleasure to work with you, David.

Sincere and abundant thanks to Rizzoli publisher Charles Miers and associate publisher of architecture David Morton for approval of this project and to editor Douglas Curran for his patience and good will through the years. I am always uplifted when speaking with you, Douglas.

Special mention must be made to two specialists upon whom I relied for reviewing my work and knowing the intricate histories of their respective towns: to Michael Redmon, Director of Research at the Santa Barbara Historical Museum (Gledhill Library) for his expertise and timely help in having particular information sent to me; and to Dennis Copeland, Historian, and Museums, Art Culture and Archives Manager for the City of Monterey, for his researched information that clarified important facts concerning the historic adobes in Monterey and review of my work.

RESOURCES

Alexander, James B. *Sonoma Valley Legacy*. Sonoma, California: Sonoma Valley Historical Society, 1986.

Benté, Vance G., Judith D. Tordoff, and Mary Hilderman-Smith. *The archaeology of the Royal Presidio of Santa Barbara Chapel Site—Phase VIII Archaeological Excavations of the Chapel Site CA-SBA-133*. Santa Barbara, California: Santa Barbara Trust for Historic Preservation, 1982.

Beresford, Hattie. "Moguls & Mansions," in *Montecito Journal Glossy Edition Magazine*, pp. 72–74, 76–78. Santa Barbara, California: Montecito Journal, Winter/Spring 2012/2013.

Burton-Carvajal, Julianne. "Pride of Place: Tales of Two Adobes," in *Noticias del Puerto de Monterey: Monterey History and Art Association Quarterly*, vol. LIII, no. 2. Monterey, California: Monterey History and Art Association, The Maritime Museum, Summer, 2004.

California State Parks and the Monterey History and Art Association. *Monterey: The First Buildings*. Monterey, California: California State Parks and the Monterey History and Arts Association, 1994.

Carr, Harry. Los Angeles: *City of Dreams*. New York, London: D. Appleton-Century Company, Incorporated, 1935.

Cole, Alexandra C. "Historic Structures/Sites Report 904 Camino Viejo, Santa Barbara, California." Santa Barbara, California: Preservation Planning Associates, July 2003.

Conard, Rebecca and Everett Weinreb, Jamie Calhoun, Shelly Bookspan. *Phase III Documentation of Historic Resources, Ennisbrook Estate/Boeseke Ranch, Montecito, California*. Santa Barbara, California: PHR Associates, July 1988.

Dahl, David. "Ennisbrooke: The Boeseke Estate," in Montecito Magazine, pp. 11–15, 17. *Montecito, California: Montecito Magazine*, Fall 1987.

Daniels, George G., editor and the editors of Time-Life Books. *The Spanish West*. Alexandria, Virginia: Time-Life Books, 1976

Gates, Dorothy L. and Jane H. Bailey. *Morrow Bay's Yesterdays: Vignettes of Our City's Lives & Times*. San Luis Obispo: Central Coast Press, 1982.

Gutiérrez, Ramón A. and Richard J. Orsi, editors. "Contested Eden: California Before the Gold Rush" in *California History, The Magazine of the California Historical Society*, vol. LXXVI, nos. 2 and 3. California: The University of California Press, Summer and Fall, 1997.

Gebhard, David. *Santa Barbara—The Creation of a New Spain in America*. Santa Barbara, California: University Art Museum, University of California Santa Barbara, 1982.

Giffen, Helen S. with Foreword by W. W. Robinson. *Casas & Courtyards: Historic Adobe Houses of California*. Oakland, Calfironia: Biobooks, 1955.

Hannaford, Donald R. and Revel Edwards with Preface by David Gebhard. *Spanish Colonial or Adobe Architecture of California 1800–1850*. Stamford, Connecticut: Architectural Book Publishing Company, Inc., 1931, 1990.

James, George Wharton. *The Old Franciscan Missions of California*. Boston: Little, Brown, and Company, 1915.

Johnson, Paul C., editor and the editorial staff of Sunset Magazine and Books. *Western Ranch Houses by Cliff May*. Santa Monica, California: Hennessey + Ingalls, 1997.

Kirker, Harold. *California's Architectural Frontier*. San Marino, California: Henry E. Huntington Library and Art Gallery, 1960 and Layton, Utah: Gibbs M. Smith, Inc. Peregrin Smith Books, 1986.

Marshall, James Wilson and Edward Gould Buffum and Edited by Doyce B. Nunis, Jr. *From Mexican Days to the Gold Rush*. Chicago: R. R. Donnelley & Sons Company, 1993.

McKowen, Ken, and Dahlynn McKowen. *Best of California's Missions, Mansions, and Museums*. Berkeley, California: Wilderness Press, 2006.

O'Connor, John F. *The Adobe Book*. Santa Fe, New Mexico: Ancient City Press, 1973.

Palmer, Christine. "The Old Adobe Buildings of Santa Barbara—From the Earth: Adobes of Santa Barbara," in *Noticias*, vol. XVIII, no. 1. Santa Barbara, California: The Santa Barbara Historical Society, Spring 2002.

Romero, Orlando and David Larkin. *Adobe: Building and Living with Earth*. Boston, New York: Houghton Mifflin Company, 1994.

Spencer, Russ. "Charmed Lives," in Santa Barbara Magazine, vol. 24, no. 3, pp. 42-45, 64–65. Santa Barbara, California: Santa Barbara Magazine, Inc., Summer, 1998.

Stevenson, Robert Louis. *The Old Pacific Capital, The New Pacific Capital*. First published 1880 and 1883 respectively. Reprinted Monterey, California: Monterey State Historic Park.

Thompson, Willard. "The Adobes of Montecito—Montecito's Nineteenth-Century Adobes and the Settlers Who Built Them—The Adobes of Montecito," in *Noticias*, vol. LIII, no. 2. Santa Barbara, California: The Santa Barbara Historical Society, 2009.

van Balgooy, Mary A., "Designer of the Dream: Cliff May and the California Ranch House," Southern California Quarterly, Vol. 86 No. 2, Summer 2004, pp. 127–144.

Witynski, Karen, and Joe P. Carr. *Casa Adobe*. Salt Lake City, Utah: Gibbs Smith, Publisher, 2001.

Woolfenden, John and Amelie Elkinton. *Cooper: Juan Bautista Rogers Cooper: Sea Captain, Adventurer, Ranchero and Early California Pioneer 1791–1872*. Pacific Grove, California: The Boxwood Press, 1983.

The picturesque rose garden at Mission San Luis Rey de Francia, established in 1798 and the largest of the California missions, is protected at its entrance by an adobe wall and brick arch. The garden compliments the striking bright white mission complex located in San Luis Rey, San Diego County, that is a California State Historic Landmark.